Dear 2nd Dad,

Thanks for being such a great father-in-law. I really think I'm lucky to be part of your family. I'm looking forward to many more vacations with you. I cant wait to go fishing, crabbing, hunting, and on and on....

Thanks for everything!

Love Andy

Photography credits: Bridgeman Art Library, page 3; Getty Images, pages 42–43, 136–37, 152, 155, 160; iStockphoto, page 83; Jupiter Images Unlimited, pages i, v, 4–5, 7, 8–9, 12, 16, 19, 23, 24–25, 26, 30–31, 33, 34, 36–37, 40, 45, 50, 54, 56–57, 60, 63, 68, 70–71, 73, 74–75, 84, 86, 88–89, 92, 96, 98–99, 101, 102, 104, 106–7, 123, 128, 130, 140, 141, 145, 148, 150–51, 162; Shutterstock, pages 10, 11, 18, 21, 32, 38, 46, 49, 52–53, 62, 64, 65, 67, 91, 95, 108–9, 111, 112, 116, 119, 120, 127, 132–33, 138, 146, 156, 158–59, 164–65; LDS Church Archives, pages 20, 134; courtesy TAGSRWC Archives, page 77; Jeri Benson, pages 121, 143; John Bytheway, pages 114, 124, 166; Jonathan Clark, page vi; Shauna Gibby, page 59; Lowell R. Hardy, page 28; Lauren Madsen, pages 14–15; Chris Schoebinger, page 78; courtesy Rita C. Smith, page 144.

Library of Congress Cataloging-in-Publication Data

Bytheway, John, 1962–
 Fishing : observations of a reel man / John Bytheway.
  p. cm.
 Includes bibliographical references.
 ISBN 978-1-60641-634-1 (hardbound : alk. paper)
 1. Fishing—Quotations, maxims, etc. 2. Fishing—Religious aspects—The Church of Jesus Christ of Latter-day Saints. 3. Quotations, English. I. Title.
 PN6084.F47B98 2010
 799.1—dc22   2009050250

Printed in China
R. R. Donnelley, Shenzhen, China

10 9 8 7 6 5 4 3 2 1

FISHING

Observations of a Reel Man

JOHN BYTHEWAY

DESERET
BOOK

SALT LAKE CITY, UTAH

ACKNOWLEDGMENTS

Thanks to Chris Schoebinger, my product director, for his encouragement; Emily Watts for her editing skills; and Shauna Gibby for her wonderful talent and hard work on the beautiful design. Thanks always to Sheri Dew and Deseret Book for sticking with me over the years.

Fishing is the chance to wash one's soul
with pure air, with the rush of a brook or with the
shimmer of the sun on blue water.

HERBERT HOOVER

The author at Wall Lake, Uinta Mountains, 1977

INTRODUCTION

Only a reel man would attempt to tackle a book about fishing. When the opportunity surfaced, I took an internal pole. My head was spinning, but I finally said, "Okay, I'll bite." With baited breath, I swallowed the opportunity hook, line, and sinker, and cast myself into the project with both waders. The net result is in your hands.

Sport fishing is also known as "angling." The word *angling* was probably derived from the shape of the "angled" fishhook, or perhaps from idea of working an "angle"—the act of trying to get something (a fish, in this case) by "sly or artful means."

As a preteen, I did few things well, but fishing was one of them. When it wasn't summertime, I'd spend hours browsing through the lures in my dad's tackle box, looking through fishing catalogs, and drawing pictures of rods and reels in church when I should have been listening.

INTERESTING DATES IN SPORT FISHING

2000 B.C.   An Egyptian mural depicts an angling scene with figures shown fishing with a rod and line.

A.D. 200   Claudius Aelianus, in his book *De Natura Animalium*, describes the Red Hackle artificial fly as follows: "They fasten red . . . wool round a hook, and fit on to the wool two feathers which grow under a cock's wattles, and which in color are like wax."

A.D. 1496   *A Treatyse of Fysshynge wyth an Angle* is published in Europe. Twelve types of artificial flies are listed, six of which are still in use today.

A.D. 1653   Izaak Walton published *The Compleat Angler,* writing, "God never did make a more calm, quiet, innocent recreation than angling."

The first men that our Saviour dear
Did choose to wait upon Him here;
Blest fishers were; and fish the last
Food was, that He on earth did taste:
I therefore strive to follow those,
Whom He to follow Him hath chose.

IZAAK WALTON, 1653

According to the book of Genesis, God said, "Let us make man in our image, after our likeness," and in the *very next phrase,* He added, "and let them have dominion over the fish of the sea" (Genesis 1:26). So I suppose it's obvious that we were made to fish!

Golf was invented around the fifteenth century. Most other sports began after the industrial revolution. But *fishing*—fishing goes way, way back to what the book of Genesis calls "the beginning."

"Three-fourths of the Earth's surface is water, and one-fourth is land. It is quite clear that the good Lord intended us to spend triple the amount of time fishing as taking care of the lawn."

CHUCK CLARK

WHY WE FISH

The average person might assume that the purpose of fishing is to catch fish. Well, not exactly. There's much, much more. Fishing is more than an occasional weekend trip; fishing is a state of mind. Which is why we go again, and again, and again.

In a nutshell, we go fishing to enjoy the beauties of nature, to build relationships with fishing companions, and to experience personal reflection and renewal. And if we're lucky enough to catch some fish on the trip, so much the better.

WHY WE FISH:
TO ENJOY NATURE

66 To go fishing is the chance to wash one's soul with pure air, with the rush of the brook, or with the shimmer of sun on blue water. It brings meekness and inspiration from the decency of nature, charity toward tackle-makers, patience toward fish, a mockery of profits and egos, a quieting of hate, a rejoicing that you do not have to decide a darned thing until next week. And it is discipline in the equality of men—for all men are equal before fish. 99

HERBERT HOOVER

66 The two best times to go fishing are when it's raining and when it's not. 99

FISHERMAN'S SAYING

"As the angler looks back, he thinks less of individual captures and days than of scenes in which he fished."

LORD GREY OF FALLONDON

> **Heaven seems a little closer**
> **in a house beside the water.**

AUTHOR UNKNOWN

> **The angling fever is a very real disease**
> **and can only be cured by the application of cold water**
> **and fresh, untainted air.**

THEODORE GORDON

> **I knew an old fisherman who said he enjoyed the times**
> **when the fish weren't biting, for then he had time to see**
> **and hear all the things he would miss if he were**
> **too busy hauling in fish.**

ARCHIBALD RUTLEDGE

When Isaiah needed to describe peace, he chose a metaphor that fisherman know all about: "O that thou hadst hearkened to my commandments! then had thy peace been as a river, and thy righteousness as the waves of the sea."

ISAIAH 48:18

David O. McKay fishing in the Tetons, 1945

*T*his life is good to us. Out of our little cabin, even between the chinks of the logs we can see the golden grain. We can hear the rippling stream. The Lord's gifts are free.

DAVID O. MCKAY

66 One of the great charms of angling is that
of all the sports, it affords the best opportunity to enjoy the
wonders and beauty of nature. **99**

J. J. MANLEY

66 Perhaps fishing is, for me,
only an excuse to be near rivers. **99**

RODERICK HAIG-BROWN

66 Fish come and go, but it is the memory of afternoons
on the stream that endures. **99**

E. DONNALL THOMAS

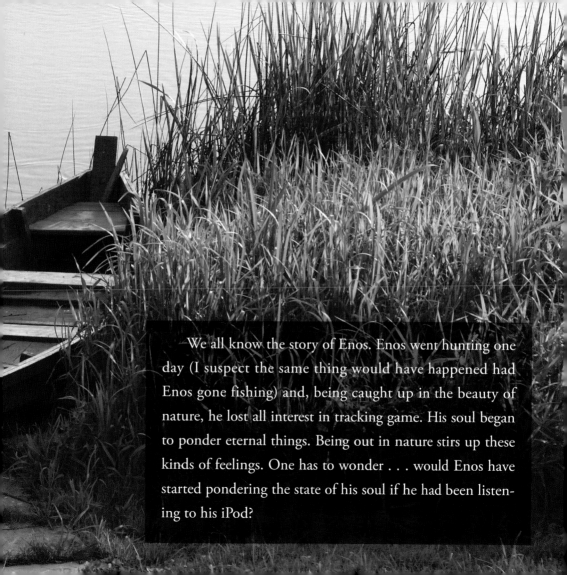

We all know the story of Enos. Enos went hunting one day (I suspect the same thing would have happened had Enos gone fishing) and, being caught up in the beauty of nature, he lost all interest in tracking game. His soul began to ponder eternal things. Being out in nature stirs up these kinds of feelings. One has to wonder . . . would Enos have started pondering the state of his soul if he had been listening to his iPod?

The angler forgets most of the fish he catches, but he does not forget the streams and lakes in which they are caught.

CHARLES K. FOX

Perspective is a perishable commodity. Fishing restores perspective. When we escape to the solitude of quiet waters, the day's fleeting troubles seem to evaporate into the mist; in the presence of Nature, spiritual order is restored.

CRISWELL FREEMAN

President Gordon B. Hinckley fishing in Alaska, 1995

President Gordon B. Hinckley reflected while visiting Glacier Bay, Alaska:

"I arose early this morning and went out on the deck. It was difficult to kneel down in the little cabin room, and so I went out on the foredeck and there stood and offered my morning prayer. I felt inspired by the beauty of the scenery—the surrounding mountains thickly covered with timber that is virgin, never having seen the woodsman's saw or axe. I reflected on the wonders of nature, these great glacial waters, icy cold, and brilliant in the sunlight."

President Hinckley was the first to catch a fish that day, and he noted: "Several cameras were trained on me. I appreciated this, because I want to take some photographs to show President Monson, who does a lot of fishing, that I too can catch a fish." Before leaving he reflected, "Being out like this is medicine for the soul."

WHY WE FISH:
RELATIONSHIPS

It was said of George H. Brimhall: "He reared his boys with a rod, but it was a fishing rod."

> 66 He that spareth his rod hateth his son . . . 99

PROVERBS 13:24

> 66 Spare the rod, and spoil the child. 99

OLD PROVERB

66 Many men go fishing all their lives without knowing
that it is not fish they are after. 99

HENRY DAVID THOREAU

66 One thing becomes clearer as one gets older and one's
fishing experience increases, and that is the paramount
importance of one's fishing companions. 99

JOHN ASHLEY-COOPER

"*Many of the most highly publicized events of my presidency are not nearly as memorable or significant in my life as fishing with my daddy.*"

JIMMY CARTER

Two Journal Entries, Opposite Perspectives

Charles Francis Adams, grandson of President John Adams, recorded in his diary: "Went fishing with my son today—a day wasted."

On that same date, Charles's son, Brooks Adams, printed in his own diary, "Went fishing with my father today—the most wonderful day of my life."

WHY WE FISH: PERSONAL RENEWAL

> **❝** I don't want to sit at the head
> table anymore. I want to go fishing. **❞**

GEORGE H. W. BUSH

> **❝** No life is so happy and so pleasant as the life
> of the well-govern'd angler. **❞**

IZAAK WALTON

> **❝** All Americans believe that they are born fishermen.
> For a man to admit a distaste for fishing would be like
> denouncing mother-love or hating moonlight. **❞**

JOHN STEINBECK

"*Lots of people committed crimes during the year who would not have done so if they had been fishing. The increase of crime is among those deprived of the regenerations that impregnate the mind and character of the fisherman.*"

HERBERT HOOVER

There is certainly something in angling that tends to produce a serenity of the mind.

WASHINGTON IRVING

As civilization, cement pavements, office buildings and radio have overwhelmed us, the need for regeneration had increased. Fishing is a sound, valid reason to go away from here to somewhere else.

HERBERT HOOVER

THE FISHERMAN
AND THE MBA

An American investment banker was standing on the pier in a small coastal village when a boat carrying just one fisherman docked. Inside the small boat were several large yellowfin tuna. The banker complimented the fisherman on the quality of his fish and asked how long it had taken to catch them.

The fisherman replied, "Only a little while."

The banker then asked, "Why didn't you stay out longer and catch more fish?"

The fisherman said, "With this I have more than enough to support my family's needs."

The banker wondered, "But what do you do with the rest of your time?"

The fisherman said, "I sleep late, fish a little, play with my children, spend some time with my wife, and stroll into the village each evening, where I relax and play guitar with my friends. I have a full and busy life."

The banker scoffed, "I am a Harvard MBA and could help you. You should spend more time fishing and, with the proceeds, buy a bigger boat. With the proceeds from the bigger boat, you could buy several boats. Eventually you would have a fleet of fishing boats. Instead of selling your catch to a middleman you could sell directly to the processor, eventually opening your own cannery. You would control the product, processing, and distribution. You would need to leave this small coastal fishing village and move to Los Angeles or New York, where you will run your ever-expanding enterprise."

The fisherman asked, "But, how long will this all take?"

To which the banker replied, "Fifteen to twenty years."

"And what then?" asked the fisherman.

The banker laughed and said, "That's the best part. When the time is right you announce an IPO and sell your company stock to the public and become very rich. You would make millions."

"Millions? Then what?"

The banker said, "Then you would retire. Move to a small coastal fishing village where you would sleep late, fish a little, play with your kids, spend time with your wife, and stroll to the village in the evenings, where you could relax and play your guitar with your friends."

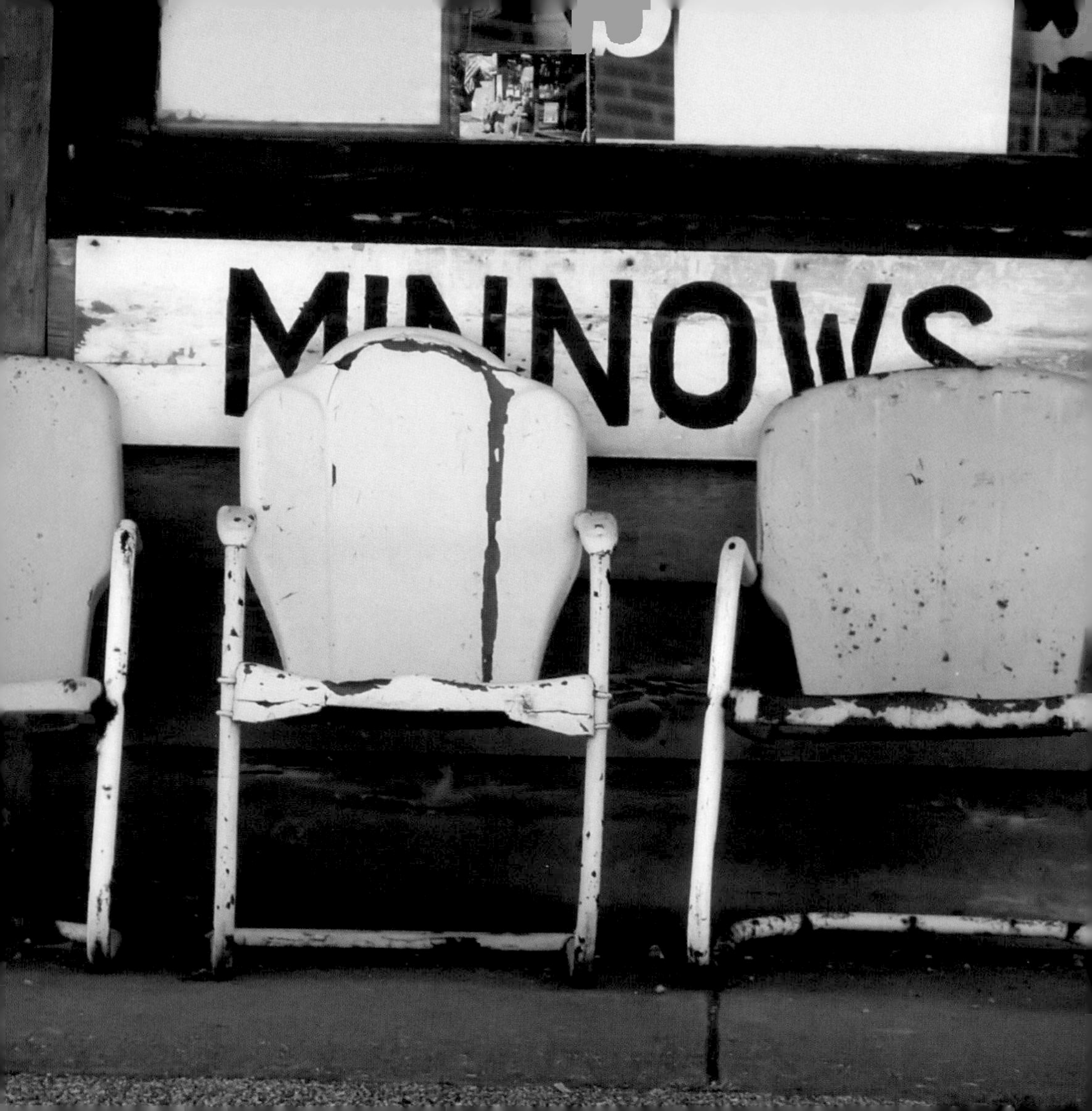
MINNOWS

" The best time to go fishing
is when you can get away. **"**

ROBERT TRAVER

" Fishing is much more than fish. Fishing is
the great occasion when we may return to
the fine simplicity of our forefathers. **"**

HERBERT HOOVER

"You will find angling to be like the virtue of humanity, which has a calmness of spirit and a world of blessing attending upon it."

Izaak Walton

> 66 Next to prayer, fishing is the most
> personal relationship of man. 99

HERBERT HOOVER

> 66 Rivers and the inhabitants of the watery elements
> are made for wise men to contemplate and for fools
> to pass by without consideration. 99

IZAAK WALTON

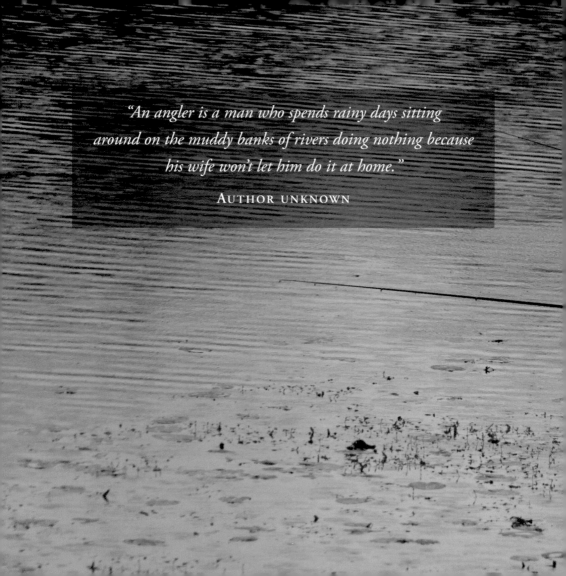

"*An angler is a man who spends rainy days sitting around on the muddy banks of rivers doing nothing because his wife won't let him do it at home.*"

AUTHOR UNKNOWN

❝ I love to fish because it is totally relaxing.
I love the water. I can concentrate and forget all my worries.
I count my blessings while fishing. **❞**

GEORGE H. W. BUSH

❝ The gods do not deduct from man's
allotted span the hours spent in fishing. **❞**

BABYLONIAN PROVERB

*P*resident George Albert Smith was invited to go on a fishing trip by Daniel Heiner, president of the Morgan Stake, to the East Canyon Reservoir. There he caught a trout weighing 5⅝ pounds. He was so delighted with this catch that he had the brethren who were with him sign a certificate to the effect that it was really a fact and not just another fish story.

Morgan, Saturday, Sept. 23/05.

This is to certify that today while fishing in the East Canyon reservoir, we saw George Albert Smith catch and land in the boat a trout weighing 5⅝ pounds, same being weighed at the Drug Store in Morgan.

(Signed) D. Heiner, W. Rich, M. Heiner.

If fishing interferes with your business, give up your business.

SPARSE GREY HACKLE

I have laid aside business and gone a-fishing.

IZAAK WALTON

FISHING TACKLE

et's do the math: You could spend around $50 for a cheap rod and reel; $20 for fishing line; another $50 for hooks, leaders, sinkers, bait, flies, waders, a net, and so on; $30 for a fishing license; and let's say $25 in gasoline to get to your destination. That's about $175.

Or, you could go to the grocery store and buy fresh trout for $6 a pound.

Okay, we admit it—fishing makes no economic sense. That being said, when do we go again?

My biggest worry is that when I'm dead and gone, my wife will sell my fishing gear for what I said I paid for it.

KOOS BRANDT

The serious fisherman understands that success on the water begins long before the first cast. Success begins with the acquisition and organization of a well-stocked tackle box. The fisherman who wishes to improve his catch must first improve his tools. In fishing, as in life, preparation is the better part of luck.

CRISWELL FREEMAN

> ❝ A good fisherman can secure many regenerative hours in winter, polishing up the rods and reels. ❞

HERBERT HOOVER

> ❝ There he stands, draped in more equipment than a telephone lineman, trying to outwit an organism with a brain no bigger than a breadcrumb, and getting licked in the process. ❞

PAUL O'NEIL

"Scholars have long known that fishing eventually turns men into philosophers. Unfortunately, it is almost impossible to buy decent tackle on a philosopher's salary."

PATRICK F. MCMANUS

BAITS AND HOOKS

Perhaps the most important life lesson from fishing comes from the point of view of the fish, and that is, don't get hooked! The devices used to catch fish are not what they appear to be—lures and artificial flies are made to look like something to eat. Bait hooks covered with worms or cheese look more like a treat than a trap.

Elder Marcus B. Nash taught: "Just as a fish in a mountain stream must be careful of the lures placed in its path to avoid being pulled away from the water, so must you and I be wise in order to avoid being pulled away from a happy, gospel-centered life. . . . Do not be deceived into even nibbling at unworthy things, for Satan stands ready to set the hook. It was the very real risk of the hook being set subtly or suddenly that led the ancient prophet Moroni—who actually saw our day (see Mormon

8:35)—to pointedly warn you and me to '*touch* not the evil gift, nor the unclean thing' (Moroni 10:30; emphasis added)."

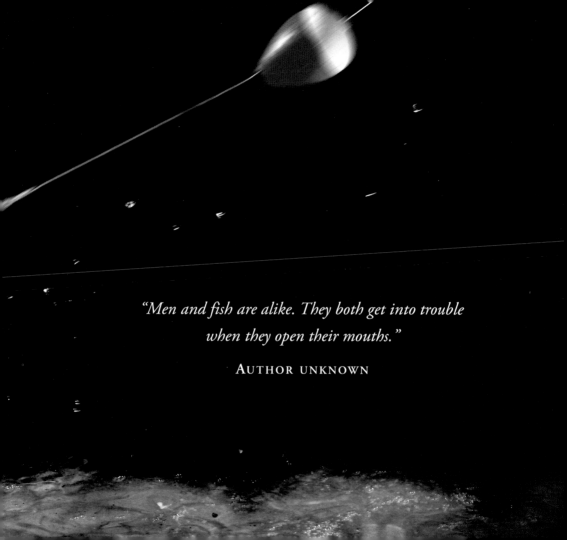

"*Men and fish are alike. They both get into trouble when they open their mouths.*"

AUTHOR UNKNOWN

OPIE: He's a good one, ain't he, Pa?

ANDY: Good? I believe never in history has anybody your size and weight landed a fish this big.

OPIE: You mean it, Pa?

ANDY: You know, if I didn't know better I would swear you was kin to Izaak Walton.

OPIE: Who's he?

ANDY: Oh, when it comes to fishin'—he's the man that wrote the book.

OPIE: I bet he wasn't better than you. I bet nobody was better than you.

ANDY: Heh-heh. I don't know. You remember Jonah? He caught hisself a whale.

OPIE: I thought the whale swallowed him.

ANDY: Well now, that's what I mean. When somebody catches a fish from the INSIDE . . . that's fishin'!

"Opie's Rival," *The Andy Griffith Show,* season three, episode 10

> **"** All the romance of trout fishing exists in the mind of the angler and is in no way shared by the fish. **"**

HAROLD F. BLAISDELL

> **"** Bait the hook well; this fish will bite. **"**

WILLIAM SHAKESPEARE,
Much Ado about Nothing, act II, scene 3

> **"** Good things come to those who bait. **"**

AUTHOR UNKNOWN

IT ALL COMES DOWN TO YOUR KNOTS

You can have a good strong fishing pole, quality fishing line, a decent lure or hook, all designed to perform perfectly, but manufactured by someone else. Holding it all together, however, is a knot tied by *you*.

When I first started fishing, I didn't know what knots to use, and I suppose I didn't think it was all that important. I tied square knots, granny knots, or whatever I could think of to attach my line to my hooks or swivels. If a square knot is good, my child's mind reasoned, then *three* square knots must be even better! So I'd just keep tying and tying, not realizing I was weakening my line by putting too many kinks in it. My early knots were a mess. More than once, I'd snag my hook on the bottom of the lake, tug too hard, and the line would break. As I reeled it in, it was clear that the line had broken at the knot. The weakest part of my rig—was me.

One day, my brother Kendrick patiently taught me what is called the "improved clinch knot." What a difference that made! I recovered many more snagged lures, hooks, and flies than before because of that knot, and I've used it ever since.

I couldn't blame my fishing pole, my reel, my lures, or my hooks for all the lost hardware. I didn't need better tackle, I just needed a smarter me. As with many things in life, blaming didn't accomplish anything, and I was often blaming the wrong thing anyway. It was what I did that held it all together.

66 Even if you've been fishing for three hours and haven't gotten anything except poison ivy and sunburn, you're still better off than the worm. 99

AUTHOR UNKNOWN

66 Something I noticed about fishing—it never works out so well for the bait. 99

BENJAMIN GATES
in the movie National Treasure

PATIENCE AND ANTICIPATION

Fishing is appealing for a variety of reasons, one of which is that it is unpredictable. Buying a fish at the store isn't nearly as much fun as hoping for one on the shore. And sometimes, one has to hope and watch and wait for a quite a while.

Many a time I've sat at attention, wide-eyed, focused on the tip of my pole, waiting for a tug on the line—often for hours at a time—but I've never been bored while fishing. (I have, however, been bored while shopping.)

One day a rather inebriated ice fisherman drilled a hole in the ice and peered into the hole, and a loud voice said, "There are no fish down there." He walked several yards away and drilled another hole and peered into it, and again the voice said, "There are no fish down there." He then walked about fifty yards away and drilled another hole, and again the voice said, "There are no fish down there."

The fisherman looked up into the sky and asked, "Lord, is that you?"

"No, you idiot," the voice said, "it's the rink manager."

Heard the one about the three beginners who went ice fishing and didn't catch anything?

By the time they cut a hole big enough for the boat to fit in, it was time to go home.

A young boy arrived to his Sunday school class late one week. His teacher, who knew that the boy was usually very prompt, asked him if anything was wrong. The boy replied no, that he was going to go fishing, but that his dad told him that he needed to go to church instead. The teacher was very impressed and asked the boy if his father had explained to him why it was more important to go to church rather than to go fishing. To which the boy replied, "Yes, ma'am, he did. My dad said that he didn't have enough bait for both of us."

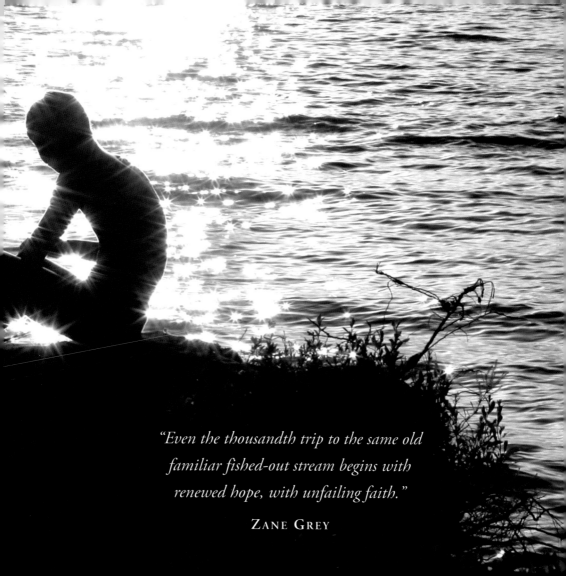

"Even the thousandth trip to the same old
familiar fished-out stream begins with
renewed hope, with unfailing faith."

ZANE GREY

66 Be patient and calm—for no one
can catch fish in anger. **99**

HERBERT HOOVER

66 Good fishing never stops. There are only times
when in some places it is better than others. **99**

GEORGE FICHTER

66 Gone fishin', be back at dark-thirty! **99**

AUTHOR UNKNOWN

> **" Fishing is boring, unless you catch an actual fish, and then it is disgusting. "**
>
> ### DAVE BARRY

> **" I love fishing. You put that line in the water and you don't know what's on the other end. Your imagination is under there. "**
>
> ### ROBERT ALTMAN

There's a fine line between fishing and just
standing on the shore like an idiot.

STEVEN WRIGHT

Persistence, for the fisherman, is a
virtue that transcends patience.

A. J. MCCLANE

The trout do not rise in the cemetery, so you better
do your fishing while you are still able.

SPARSE GREY HACKLE

WE DIDN'T CATCH A THING

> **The fishing was good; it was the catching that was bad.**
>
> A.K. BEST

> **It has always been my private conviction that any man who pits his intelligence against a fish and loses has it coming.**
>
> JOHN STEINBECK

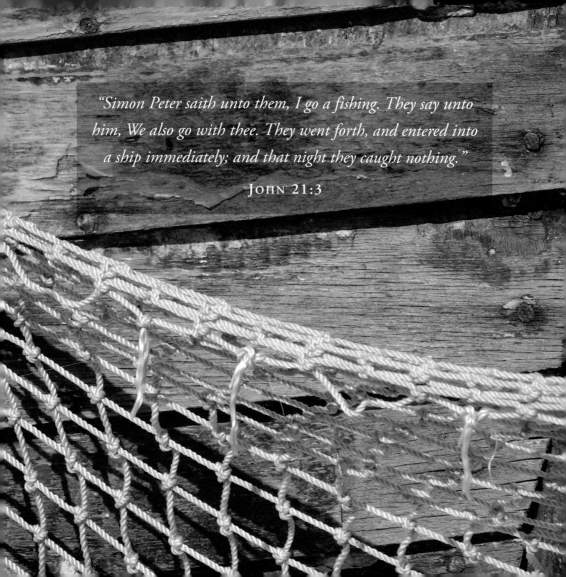

"Simon Peter saith unto them, I go a fishing. They say unto him, We also go with thee. They went forth, and entered into a ship immediately; and that night they caught nothing."

JOHN 21:3

I have fished through fishless days that I
remember happily without regret.

RODERICK HAIG-BROWN

No matter how good a man gets at fishing,
he'll never land every fish he hooks.

A. J. MCCLANE

> **When there are no fish in one spot, cast your hook in another.**

CHINESE PROVERB

> **There was never an angler who lived but that there was a fish capable of taking the conceit out of him.**

ZANE GREY

> **A fish on the hook is better than ten in the brook.**

FISHERMAN'S SAYING

*O*ne early morning in July, President Marion G. Romney went fishing with his son on the Provo River. President Romney had been so busy he had not acquired a license. When the day was over he dryly recorded, "I couldn't fish because I didn't have a license or fishing gear, but we both caught the same number of fish anyway."

"*The fishers also shall mourn, and all they that cast angle into the brooks shall lament, and they that spread nets upon the waters shall languish.*"

Isaiah 19:8

GIVE A MAN A FISH

"Give a man a fish and he will eat for a day; teach him how to fish and he will eat for a lifetime."

ANCIENT PROVERB

VARIATIONS ON THE ANCIENT PROVERB:

"Give a man a fish and he will eat for a day. Teach him how to fish and he will sit in a boat and drink beer all day."

AUTHOR UNKNOWN

"Give a man a fish and he has food for a day; teach him how to fish and you can get rid of him for the entire weekend."

ZENNA SCHAFFER

"Give a man a fish; you have fed him for today.
Teach a man to fish and you can sell him fishing equipment."

AUTHOR UNKNOWN

"Give a man a fish and he'll eat for a day.
Teach him to fly fish and he'll move to Montana."

AUTHOR UNKNOWN

"Give a man a fish; you have fed him for today.
Teach a man to fish and you will not have to listen to his
incessant whining about how hungry he is."

AUTHOR UNKNOWN

"If you wish to be happy for eight days, kill your pig and eat it.
If you wish to be happy for a lifetime, learn to fish."

CHINESE PROVERB

ANY LUCK? WHAT ARE YOU USING?

One question familiar to fisherman is this: "Any luck?" These two words are routinely spoken by other anglers as they pass by your fishing hole, looking for one of their own. If you answer, "Yeah, I've gotten a few," their next question will bounce back in a hurry: "What are you using?"

In fishing and in life, it's not a bad idea to ask the same two questions. We ask about those we admire, what makes them what they are? Is it luck? Skill? A little of both? Also, what are they using? What are they doing to get what they're getting? Isn't that why we study the lives of people we respect? We want to know what they were doing and how they did it, so that we can do it too.

Author Jim Rohn suggests that when you encounter anyone's name in the scriptures, it's usually either an example or a warning. An example says, "Do what this one did," while a warning says, "Don't do what this one did."

"And if *your* name ever ends up in someone's book," he warns, "make sure it's used as an example and not a warning!"

" Luck affects everything; let your hook always be cast. In the stream where you least expect it, there will be a fish. **"**

OVID

" Bragging may not bring happiness, but no man having caught a large fish goes home through an alley. **"**

AUTHOR UNKNOWN

John, Ashley, and Kim Bytheway at Trial Lake, Uinta Mountains

It was a great moment in my marriage. My wife, Kim, who had never been fishing before, was sitting on the other end of the canoe, trolling a "triple-teaser" for small trout in one of my favorite fishing spots. As morning turned into afternoon, Kim pulled her fourth fish into the canoe and said with a grin, "I could do this all day!" *Yippee!* I thought inside, *I have a wife who is now hooked on fishing!* Which means I'll be dusting off the tackle box again this spring.

Thomas S. Monson

When I was fourteen years old, our troop went to Big Cottonwood Canyon on a Scout outing. After setting up camp, our leader said to me, "Monson, you like to fish. I'm giving you two fishing flies—a black gnat and a white miller. Now you catch enough fish to feed this troop for the next three days, and I'll pick all of you up on Saturday." He departed. I never questioned his charge. I knew if I did my part I'd catch the fish and feed the troop. And I did. I was a man before I realized it just isn't proper for the Scoutmaster to bail out on the boys. But what a learning experience it was for us.

Man can learn a lot from fishing. When the fish are biting, no problem in the world is big enough to be remembered.

O. A. BATTISTA

This one makes a net, this one stands and wishes. Would you like to bet which one gets the fishes?

AUTHOR UNKNOWN

"A thousand fishing trips go by, indistinguishable from one another, and then suddenly one comes along that is fatefully perfect."

A. J. McClane

Kendrick Bytheway, Mike Moffit, and John Bytheway after a
"fatefully perfect" day on the Provo River

STRANGER: Any luck? Catch any fish?

FISHERMAN: Did I! I took thirty out of this stream this morning.

STRANGER: Do you know who I am? I'm the game warden.

FISHERMAN: Do you know who I am? I'm the biggest liar in the country.

The author at Wall Lake, Uinta Mountains, 1977

THE EXPERIENCE
OF OTHERS

They say that wise men learn from experience, but *super*wise men learn from others' experience.

My Scout troop was camping on the south side of Wall Lake in the Uinta Mountains. We noticed a fish that kept surfacing near a partially submerged stump only about twenty feet from shore. Most of the troop spent half the day trying to catch that fish, without success.

My brother and I had a book called *The Trout Fisherman's Bible,* which, I'm embarrassed to say, we read with a lot more gusto than our real Bible. The wise fisherman who authored that book taught me that trout can see fishermen on the shore, and that they can feel vibrations, like those made by a bunch of teenagers stomping around on the bank.

About sunset, long after the others had given up, I employed the tactics taught in *The Trout Fisherman's Bible.* I crept softly along the shore in crouched position. I didn't have a fly rod, so, using my spinning tackle, I rigged up a clear bubble, a four-foot leader, and a gray-hackle peacock artificial fly. I cast my fly well beyond the area where the fish was surfacing and reeled my line slowly toward that tree stump. Nothing happened on my first attempt, but on my second try, the fish rose to the surface, took my fly—and the fight was on. I caught him!

Yes, I caught the trout, but I also learned a lesson. Whatever you're trying to do, someone has written a book about it. Someone knows more about it than I do. Be superwise! Today I read my real Bible more than my *Fisherman's Bible,* and I hope I never miss a chance to learn from the experience of others.

FLY-FISHING

Fly-fishing is the high end of angling. It raises fishing to an art form. If you've ever seen a fly fisherman casting his line, you'll know what I mean. Am I a fly fisherman? Well, let's put it this way. I have a fly rod. Beyond that, well, I'm not quite there yet. I've tried, and I've cast my line, and I've unintentionally put knots in my leader, and I've snagged a few willows. I've even had a few trout roll for my fly, but, as of yet, I haven't caught any on my fly rod. But I'm not giving up. The appeal and beauty of fly-fishing is just too strong, and I'll be back to try again someday.

66 In our family, there was no clear line between religion and fly-fishing. **99**

NORMAN MACLEAN
First line of "A River Runs Through It"

66 If fishing is like religion, then fly-fishing is high church. **99**

TOM BROKAW

> **"** The man who coined the phrase 'Money can't buy happiness' never bought himself a good fly rod! **"**
>
> REG BAIRD

> **"** To paraphrase a deceased patriot, I regret that I have only one life to give to my fly-fishing. **"**
>
> ROBERT TRAVER

66 Somebody just back of you while you are fishing
is as bad as someone looking over your shoulder
while you write a letter to your girl. 99

ERNEST HEMINGWAY

66 There is no greater fan of fly-fishing than the worm. 99

PATRICK F. MCMANUS

Wilford Woodruff,
July 8, 1847
Near Fort Bridger, Wyoming

As soon as I got my breakfast I riged up my trout rod that I had brought with me from Liverpool, fixed my reel, line, & Artificial fly & went to one of the brooks close by Camp. . . . I went & flung my fly onto the [water] And it being the first time that I ever tried the Artificial fly in America, or ever saw it tried, I watched it as it floated upon the water with as much intens interest As Franklin did his kite when he tried to draw lightning from the skies. And as recieved great Joy when he saw electricity . . . descend on his kite string in like manner was I highly gratifyed when I saw the nimble trout dart my fly hook himself & run away with the line but I soon worried him out & drew him to shore & I fished two or three hours, including morning & evening & I cought twelve in all.

"It is not difficult to learn how to cast; but it is difficult to learn not to snap the flies off at every throw."

CHARLES DUDLEY WARNER

> **❝** These brook trout will strike any fly you present,
> provided you don't get close enough to present it. **❞**

DICK BLALOCK

> **❝** When the beginner can cast his fly into his hat,
> eight times out of ten, at forty feet, he is a fly fisher;
> and so far as casting is concerned, a good one. **❞**

JAMES A. HENSHALL

> **❝** What a tourist terms a plague of insects,
> the fly fisher calls a great hatch. **❞**

PATRICK F. MCMANUS

Unless one can enjoy himself fishing with the fly, even when his efforts are unrewarded, he loses much real pleasure. More than half the intense enjoyment of fly-fishing is derived from the beautiful surroundings, the satisfaction felt from being in the open air, the new lease of life secured thereby, and the many, many pleasant recollections of all one has seen, heard, and done.

CHARLES F. ORVIS

66 The one great ingredient in successful fly-fishing is patience. The man whose fly is always on the water has the best chance. There is always a chance of a fish or two, no matter how hopeless it looks. You never know what may happen in fly-fishing. 99

FRANCIS FRANCIS

66 The great charm of fly-fishing is that we are always learning. 99

THEODORE GORDON

66 The artificial fly is far the best thing now known to fish trout with. 99

WILFORD WOODRUFF

J oseph F. Smith and Hyrum M. Smith attended a stake conference in Coalville, Utah, August 6, 1907. While there, President Smith went fishing with local stake president Frank Taylor on the Weber River. Charles R. Savage took this photo of President Smith with a creel full of fish.

RESPECT

The more time fishermen spend in the beauties of nature, the more they come to respect it. Devoted fishermen don't litter, they don't pollute the water, and they don't kill for the fun of it. Some practice "catch and release" angling, and return their fish to the water to live another season and be enjoyed by someone else.

Fishing has a lot of spiritual meanings. A true fisherman enjoys it. It's not for money. I think Heavenly Father only made so many true fishermen—those who take it to heart and care about why the fish are there and who put them there. You know, we fish with faith, not with greed. I know from my fishing experiences that if you put good in you will get good out. The Savior spoke often about fishermen. There are so many lessons to be learned in fishing.

GORDON HAGLUND

> **❝** A good game fish is too valuable to
> be caught only once. **❞**

LEE WULFF

> **❝** One of the great qualities of fishing
> is that it is non-competitive. **❞**

JOHN ATHERTON

"In any sport, the anticipation of what might happen is almost as important as what actually happens."

BOB COSTAS

"We Thank Thee for This Food"

Two missionaries, Elder B. and Elder M., were working without purse or scrip and hadn't eaten in more than twenty-four hours. They were traversing some unfriendly farm country and didn't dare ask any of the locals for food. Finally Elder M. suggested they kneel down and ask the Lord to help them find something to eat. As they stood following the prayer, Elder M. noticed a trout rising for a fly in a nearby brook. "Oh, for a fishing pole!" he said. Elder B. replied, "What's wrong with the one you have in your hand?"

The two missionaries made some fishing line out of thread, bent a safety pin into a fishhook, and attached the makeshift gear to Elder M.'s umbrella. After finding a worm under a *stump and putting it on the "hook," Elder M. crept up to the stream, dangled it in the water, and let it float downstream. WHAM! The fish took the worm, and Elder M. pulled back hard on the umbrella. The trout sailed over his head, off the hook, and onto the bank. Elder B. was laughing, but he had tears of gratitude in his eyes. "Find another worm!" he said.*

Soon, Elder M. had caught five more, and in a few short minutes six trout were broiling over a fire. When those missionaries said, "Father in Heaven, we thank thee for this food," it came from the heart.

Who were these resourceful elders? Elder Reuel J. Bawden and Elder Truman G. Madsen.

FISHERS OF MEN

"And Jesus said unto them, Come ye after me, and I will make you to become fishers of men" (Mark 1:17).

Fishing is an interesting, peaceful, even joyous sport. If this age-old summer pastime is capable of bringing such joy to fishermen, imagine the joy that would come to someone who catches men and brings them to Christ!

The Savior promised, "And if it so be that you should labor all your days in crying repentance unto this people, and bring, save it be one soul unto me, how great shall be your joy with him in the kingdom of my Father!

"And now, if your joy will be great with one soul that you have brought unto me into the kingdom of my Father, how great will be your joy if you should bring many souls unto me!" (D&C 18:15–16).

Simon Peter had quite a day—one hundred and fifty-three fish! After they had eaten, the resurrected Lord looked at the remainder of Peter's catch and asked, "Lovest thou me more than these?" (John 21:15).

Peter left his nets, and became a "fisher of men." Today, some senior couples spend their retirement years fishing, while others, with love for the Lord and faith in his promises, leave their nets and become fishers of men.

The contrast thus presented between their [the disciples'] former vocation and their new calling is strikingly forceful. Theretofore they had caught fish, and the fate of the fish was death; thereafter they were to draw men—to a life eternal.

JAMES E. TALMAGE

Whereas hunters pursue their quarry, assailing them with slings and arrows, the fishers of men are to use the methods of "persuasion, long-suffering, gentleness, meekness, and love unfeigned" (D&C 121:41). It is well to remember that fishing requires that the fish must take some of the initiative in order to swim into the gospel net, therein finding the eternal meaning of life.

SPENCER J. CONDIE

66 There are always greater fish than you have caught,

always the lure of greater task and achievement,

always the inspiration to seek, to endure, to find. 99

ZANE GREY

66 Behold, I will send for many fishers, saith

the Lord, and they shall fish them. 99

JEREMIAH 16:16

"As line spins off the reel of life, the years weave a crazy quilt pattern. And it is strange how the seemingly great things become small and the small things become great."

RALPH BANDINI

Ashley and Andrew Bytheway at Trial Lake, August 2007

SOURCES

p. v. Herbert Hoover, in Criswell Freeman, editor, *The Fisherman's Guide to Life* (Walnut Grove Press, 1996), 23.

p. 2. *Encyclopaedia Britannica,* 1970, s.v. "Fishing," 370–71; *World Book Encyclopedia,* 1967, s.v. "Fishing," 152, 156.

p. 4. Izaak Walton, *The Compleat Angler* (The Modern Library, 1996), 88.

p. 8. Chuck Clark, www.quotegarden.com/fishing.html and numerous other internet sources.

p. 13. Herbert Hoover, www.hooverassociation.org/hoover/quotes.php.

p. 15. Lord Gray of Fallondon, in *Fisherman's Guide to Life,* 95.

p. 17. Theodore Gordon, www.wvangler.com/fishingquotes.htm and numerous other internet sources; Archibald Rutledge, in *Fisherman's Guide to Life,* 78.

p. 21. David O. McKay, "Widening Horizons," *Improvement Era,* vol. xxxii (August 1939), no. 8, n.p.

p. 22. J. J. Manley, in *Fisherman's Guide to Life,* 84; Roderick Haig-Brown, www.wvangler.com/fishingquotes.htm and numerous other internet sources; E. Donnall Thomas, www.fourseasonsanglers.com and numerous other internet sources.

p. 27. Charles K. Fox, sunriveranglers.org/newsletters/200712.pdf; Criswell Freeman, *Fisherman's Guide to Life,* 13.

p. 29. Gordon B. Hinckley, in Sheri L. Dew, *Go Forward with Faith: The Biography of Gordon B. Hinckley* (Deseret Book, 1996), 523–24.

p. 31. In Raymond Brimhall Holbrook and Esther Hamilton Holbrook, *The Tall Pine Tree: The Life and Work of George H. Brimhall,* cited in *Ensign,* November 1994, 53–54.

p. 35. Henry David Thoreau, www.quotegarden.com/fishing.html and numerous other internet sources; John Ashley-Cooper, in *Fisherman's Guide to Life,* 20.

p. 37. Jimmy Carter, www.wvangler.com/fishingquotes.htm and numerous other internet sources.

p. 39. Cited in "Doing Simple Things Brings Great Blessings," *LDS Church News,* October 8, 1994.

p. 41. George H.W. Bush, www.westslopefly.com/pages/quotes.cfm and numerous other internet sources; Izaak Walton, *The Compleat Angler,* 112; John Steinbeck, chatna.com/author/steinbeck.htm and numerous other internet sources.

p. 43. Herbert Hoover, www.poemofquotes .com/funny-quotes/fishing-quotes.php and numerous other internet sources.

p. 44. Washington Irving, www.quotegarden .com/fishing.html; Herbert Hoover, in *Fisherman's Guide to Life,* 110.

pp. 47–49. "The Fisherman and the MBA," story based on www.noogenesis.com/pineapple/ fisherman.html and numerous other internet sources.

p. 51. Robert Traver, www.tofinofishing.com/ whoweare/our-philosophy.php and numerous other internet sources; Herbert Hoover, www.stillwaterflyfish.com/fishingquotes.htm and numerous other internet sources.

p. 52. Izaak Walton, www.wvangler.com/ FishingQuotes.htm and numerous other internet sources.

p. 55. Herbert Hoover, www.stillwaterflyfish .com/fishingquotes.htm and numerous other internet sources; Izaak Walton, quoting an "ingenious Spaniard" thought to be John Valdesso, in *The Compleat Angler,* 28.

p. 58. George H. W. Bush, cited in *Chicken Soup for the Fisherman's Soul* (Health Communications Inc., 2004), 86.

p. 61. Preston Nibley, *Presidents of the Church* (Deseret Book, 1974), 274–75.

p. 62. Sparse Grey Hackle (pen name of Alfred W. Miller), in *Fisherman's Guide to Life,* 19; Izaak Walton, *The Compleat Angler,* xxxvi.

p. 66. Koos Brandt, www.toomanyquotes.com/ people/koos-brandt, and numerous other internet sources; Criswell Freeman, *Fisherman's Guide to Life,* 53.

p. 69. Herbert Hoover, www.westslopefly.com/pages/quotes.cfm and numerous other internet sources; Paul O'Neil, www.mackdays.com/ fishing_quotes.htm and numerous other internet sources.

p. 71. Patrick F. McManus, *Never Sniff a Gift Fish* (Holt Paperbacks, 1984), 20.

pp. 72–73. Marcus B. Nash, "The Great Plan of Happiness," *Ensign,* November 2006, 49–50.

p. 76. "Opie's Rival," *The Andy Griffith Show,* season three, episode 10.

p. 79. Harold F. Blaisdell, www.wvangler.com/ fishingquotes.htm and numerous other internet sources; William Shakespeare, *Much Ado about Nothing,* act II, scene 3.

p. 82. Benjamin Gates, in the movie *National Treasure,* Walt Disney Pictures, 2005.

p. 88. Zane Grey, www.westslopefly.com/ pages/quotes.cfm and numerous other internet sources.

p. 90. Herbert Hoover, www.fishinglegends.com and numerous other internet sources; George Fichter, www.anamericanangler.com/ greatquotes.html.

p. 93. Dave Barry, www.brainyquote.com and numerous other internet sources; Robert Altman, www.realsreels.com/ Quotesfishing.aspx.

p. 94. Steven Wright, www.quotationspage.com/quote/1244.html and numerous other internet sources; A. J. McClane, in *Fisherman's Guide to Life,* 71; Sparse Grey Hackle (pen name of Alfred W. Miller), www.stillwaterflyfish.com/ fishingquotes.htm and numerous other internet sources.

p. 97. A. K. Best, www.wvangler.com/ fishingquotes.htm; John Steinbeck, www.fishwlb.com/jokes.html and numerous other internet sources.

p. 100. Roderick Haig-Brown, www.westslopefly.com/pages/Quotes.cfm and numerous other internet sources; A. J. McClane, in *Fisherman's Guide to Life,* 124.

p. 103. Zane Grey, in *Fishermans' Guide to Life,* 125.

p. 105. Marion G. Romney, in F. Burton Howard, *Marion G. Romney: His Life and Faith* (Bookcraft, 1988), 156.

p. 108. Zenna Schaffer, http://www.amusing quotes.com/h/s/Zenna_Schaffer_1.htm.

p. 111. Jim Rohn, www.jimrohn.com.

p. 113. Ovid, in *Fisherman's Guide to Life,* 80.

p. 117. Thomas S. Monson, "The Upward Reach," *Ensign,* November 1993, 47.

p. 118. O. A. Battista, in *Fisherman's Guide to Life,* 37.

p. 120. A. J. McClane, in *Fisherman's Guide to Life,* 77.

p. 122. Jack M. Lyon, Jay A. Parry, and Linda R. Gundry, eds., *Best-Loved Humor of the LDS People* (Deseret Book, 1999), 104.

p. 131. Norman Maclean, *A River Runs Through It* (University of Chicago Press, 1976), 1; Tom Brokaw, www.granddaddyflyfishing .com/sayings.htm and numerous other internet sources.

p. 132. Reg Baird, www.flyfishingjoy.com/ Fly_Fishing_Quotes.html and numerous other internet sources; Robert Traver, www .inspirational-quotes-cafe.com/funny-fishing-quote.html and numerous other internet sources.

p. 133. Ernest Hemingway, http://quotations book.com/quote/15091; Patrick F. McManus, www.flyfishingjoy.com/ Fly_Fishing_Quotes.html and numerous other internet sources.

p. 135. Wilford Woodruff, in William H. Slaughter and Michael N. Landon, *Trail of Hope* (Deseret Book, 1997), 164–65. Original spelling and punctuation preserved.

p. 137. Charles Dudley Warner, in Edward Windsor Kemble and William Dean Howells, *Mark Twain's Library of Humor* (Charles L. Webster & Co., 1888), 12.

p. 139. Dick Blalock, www.alabiff.com/ quotes_fishing.html; James A. Henshall, www.wvangler.com/fishingquotes.htm; Patrick A. McManus, www.poemofquotes .com/funny-quotes/fishing-quotes.php.

p. 140. Charles F. Orvis, www.napavalleyfly fishers.org/quotes.html.

p. 142. Francis Francis, www.wvangler.com/ fishingquotes.htm and numerous other internet sources; Theodore Gordon,

http://www.smokyonthefly.com/guide.html; Wilford Woodruff, Journal of Wilford Woodruff, July 8, 1847, 3:225.

p. 145. Story of Joseph F. Smith in Richard Neitzel Holzapfel and William W. Slaughter, *Prophets of the Latter Days* (Deseret Book, 2003), 83.

p. 147. Gordon Haglund, "Teachers 'Fish with Faith,'" *LDS Church News,* July 9, 1988.

p. 149. Lee Wulff, www.wvangler.com/ fishingquotes.htm; John Atherton, in *Fisherman's Guide to Life,* 96.

p. 150. Bob Costas, in *Chicken Soup for the Fisherman's Soul,* 2.

p. 153–54. Story based on Truman G. Madsen, "A Prayer and an Answer," *Improvement Era,* March 1948, 151.

p. 161. James E. Talmage, *Jesus the Christ* (Deseret Book, 1976), 198–99; Spencer J. Condie, *In Perfect Balance* (Bookcraft, 1993), 87.

p. 163. Zane Grey, www.westslopefly.com/ pages/quotes.cfm.

p. 165. Ralph Bandini, in *Fisherman's Guide to Life,* 113.